CAPTAIN
AMERICA
ORIGINS

CAPTAIN AMERICA

ORIGINS

"The Legend Reborn"
Writer: **Scott Gray**
Artist: **Craig Rousseau**
Colorist: **Chris Sotomayor**
Letterer: **Dave Sharpe**

"Spy for the Cameras"
Writer: **Roger Langridge**
Artist: **Craig Rousseau**
Colorist: **Chris Sotomayor**
Letterer: **Dave Sharpe**
Cover Artist: **Clayton Henry & Guru eFX**
Editor: **Nathan Cosby**
Consulting Editor: **Ralph Macchio**

"Web of Deceit"
Writer: **Scott Gray**
Penciler: **Matteo Lolli**
Inker: **Christian Vecchia**
Colorist: **Sotocolor**
Letterer: **Dave Sharpe**
Cover Artist: **Clayton Henry & Guru eFX**

"If This Be P.R.O.D.O.K.!"
Writer: **Roger Langridge**
Artist: **Craig Rousseau**
Colorist: **Sotocolor**
Letterer: **Dave Sharpe**
Cover Artist: **Clayton Henry & Guru eFX**
Editor: **Nathan Cosby**
Consulting Editor: **Ralph Macchio**

"Stars, Stripes and Spiders!"
Writer: **Todd Dezago**
Penciler: **Lou Kang**
Inker: **Pat Davidson**
Colorist: **Digital Rainbow**
Letterer: **Dave Sharpe**
Editor: **John Barber**
Consulting Editors: **Mackenzie Cadenhead**
& **Ralph Macchio**

"The Living Legend"
Writer: **Roger Stern**
Artist: **John Byrne**
Colorist: **Bob Sharen**
Letterer: **Joe Rosen**
Editor: **Jim Salicrup**

Captain America created by **Joe Simon and Jack Kirby**

Collection Editor: **Cory Levine**
Editorial Assistants: **James Emmett & Joe Hochstein**
Assistant Editors: **Matt Masdeu, Alex Starbuck & Nelson Ribeiro**
Editors, Special Projects: **Jennifer Grünwald & Mark D. Beazley**
Senior Editor, Special Projects: **Jeff Youngquist**
Senior Vice President of Sales: **David Gabriel**

Editor in Chief: **Joe Quesada**
Publisher: **Dan Buckley**
Executive Producer: **Alan Fine**

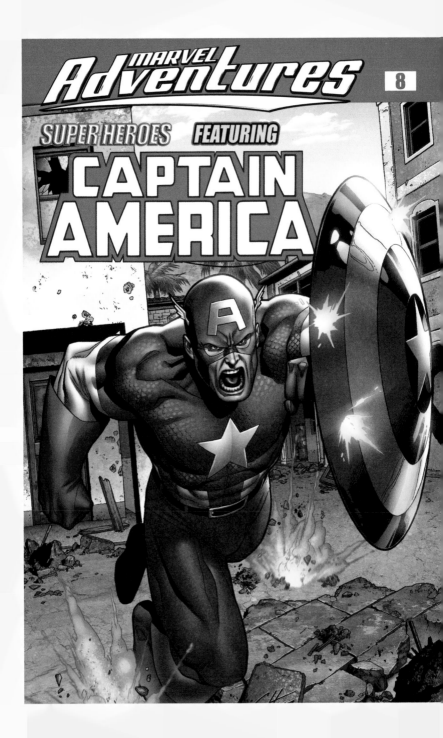

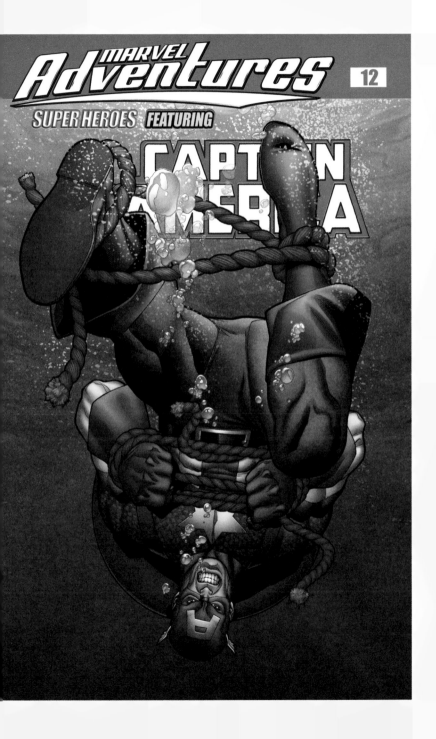

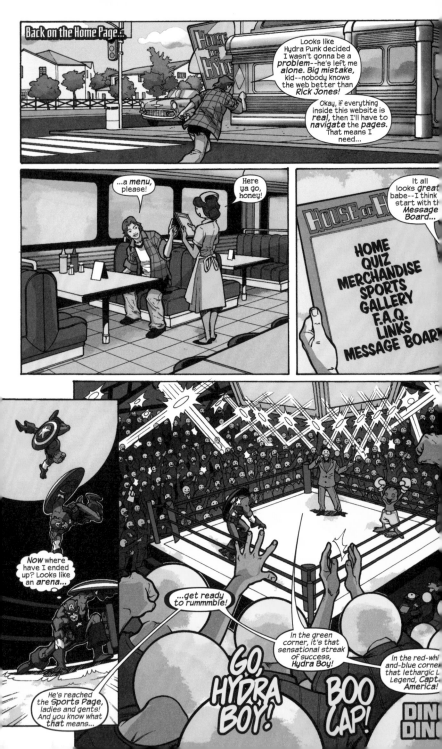

BITTEN BY AN IRRADIATED SPIDER, WHICH GRANTED HIM INCREDIBLE ABILITIES, **PETER PARKER** LEARNED THE ALL-IMPORTANT LESSON, THAT WITH GREAT POWER THERE MUST ALSO COME GREAT RESPONSIBILITY. AND SO HE BECAME THE AMAZING **SPIDER-MAN** AND

AMERICA'S WORLD WAR II SUPER SOLDIER, YOUNG **STEVE ROGERS** WAS FROZEN FOR DECADES IN A BLOCK OF ICE! REVIVED, ROGERS TODAY CONTINUES TO BATTLE AS THE RED, WHITE AND BLUE SYMBOL OF FREEDOM-- **CAPTAIN AMERICA** IN

STARS, STRIPES, AND SPIDERS!

Your *eyes* are not playing *tricks* on you, O' Mighty *Marvelite!* In his short yet *remarkable* career, Spidey has crossed paths with some pretty *colorful characters* (to say the least)...

...but *never* before has he stood side-by-side with the red-white-and-blue-clad *champion* of World War II, *Captain America!*

And if the ghastly Grey Gargoyle has anything to say about it, Spidey may be holding that honor for all eternity!

LEN WEIN & GIL KANE **INSPIRATION** TODD DEZAGO **SCRIPT** LOU KANG **PENCILS**
PAT DAVIDSON **INKS** DAVE SHARPE **LETTERS** DIGITAL RAINBOW **COLORS** JOHN BARBER **EDITOR**
MACKENZIE CADENHEAD & RALPH MACCHIO **CONSULTING EDITORS** JOE QUESADA **EDITOR-IN-CHIEF** DAN BUCKLEY **PUBLISHER**

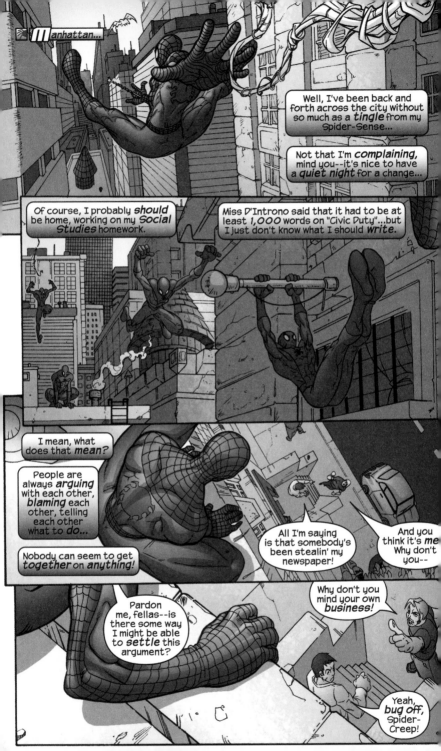

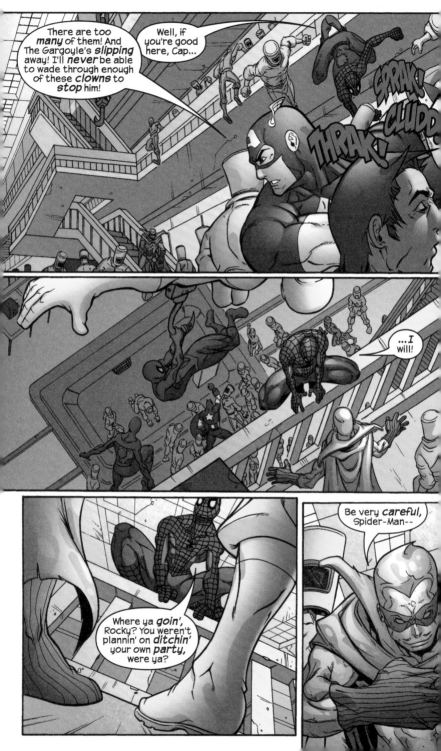

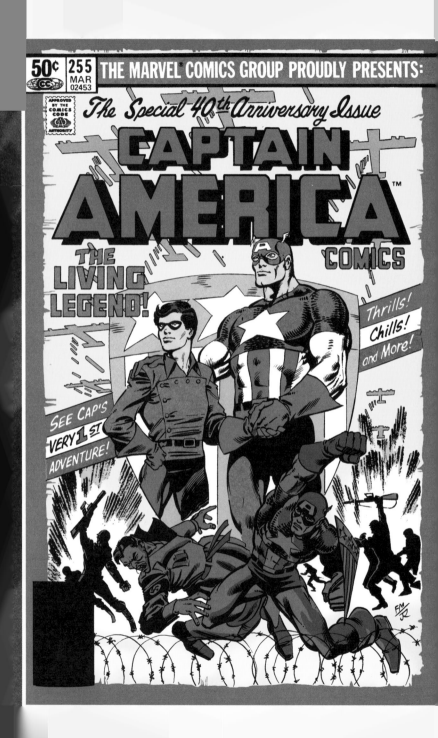

"IN A MATTER OF MINUTES, THE GLEAMING HOPE OF *OPERATION: REBIRTH* CAME TO AN ABRUPT END.

"THE SECRET OF THE SUPER-SOLDIER SERUM APPARENTLY DIED WITH DR. ERSKINE, WHO HAD NEVER COMMITTED THE FULL FORMULA TO PAPER.

"AS FOR 'AGENT CLEMSON,' A MAN WE LATER IDENTIFIED AS NAZI ASSASSIN *HEINZ KRUGER*...HE, TOO, PAID THE FINAL PRICE.

"KNOCKED INTO THE VITA-RAY DEVICE'S *ELECTRICAL OMNI-VERTER* POWER SOURCE BY ROGERS' PUNCH, HE SCRAMBLED TO FREE HIMSELF--

"--AND IN DOING SO, HE GRABBED HOLD OF THE OMNI-VERTER'S HIGH-VOLTAGE TERMINALS ...AND WAS INSTANTLY ELECTROCUTED!

"THE SUPER-SOLDIER SERUM WORKED...ROGERS WAS LIVING PROOF OF THAT! BUT WE COULD NEVER PRODUCE ANOTHER MAN LIKE HIM..."

...AND SO ENDED OUR BOLD EXPERIMENT.

THE WORLD IS POORER FOR THE LOSS OF ABRAHAM ERSKINE!

YES, SIR. BUT HE DID LEAVE US AN IMPORTANT LEGACY--

--IN THE "REBORN" STEVE ROGERS. AS YOU KNOW, ACTING UPON GENERAL PHILLIPS' ADVISEMENT, ROGERS BECAME THE CORNERSTONE OF...*PROJECT: SUPER-SOLDIER!*

AS *THIS* DOSSIER SHOWS, MR. PRESIDENT--

PROJECT: SUPER-SOLDIER

TOP SECRET

"--SHORTLY AFTER DR. ERSKINE'S TRAGIC DEATH, ROGERS WAS PUT INTO A SPECIAL TRAINING PROGRAM, TO TEACH HIM HOW TO BEST USE HIS NEW BODY!

"FOR THREE MONTHS, HE WORKED OUT WITH THE GREATEST BOXERS, WRESTLERS, BODY BUILDERS, AND GYMNASTS THE FREE WORLD HAD TO OFFER! AND WHATEVER TIME NOT SPENT IN PHYSICAL TRAINING WAS SPENT IN LEARNING THE FINE POINTS OF MILITARY STRATEGY AND TACTICS.

"THIS WAS PERSONALLY SUPERVISED BY GENERAL PHILLIPS!

BUT ONE NIGHT, JUST A FEW MONTHS LATER, YOUNG JAMES BUCHANAN BARNES STUMBLED ACROSS ONE OF HIS NATION'S MOST GUARDED SECRETS, AND CHANGED HIS LIFE FOR ALL TIME!

PLEDGING TO KEEP STEVE'S SECRET, BUCKY UNDERWENT MONTHS OF INTENSIVE TRAINING, BECOMING CAP'S PARTNER IN THE WAR AGAINST TYRANNY!

THEN CAME THAT AWFUL DAY... *DECEMBER 7TH, 1941.* AND AMERICA WAS TRULY AT WAR!

BEFORE THE YEAR HAD ENDED, CAP AND BUCKY FOUND THEMSELVES ALLIED WITH A GROUP OF POWERFUL BEINGS... A SUPER-TEAM WHICH WINSTON CHURCHILL DUBBED *THE INVADERS!*

FOR FOUR INCREDIBLE YEARS, THEY BATTLED THE NAZI MENACE--

--IN ALL OF ITS BIZARRE FORMS!

THEN, IN THE WAR'S FINAL DAYS, TRAGEDY STRUCK AGAIN! WHILE TRYING TO STOP A RUNAWAY, EXPERIMENTAL DRONE PLANE, CAP AND BUCKY WERE CAUGHT ON THE SPEEDING CRAFT AS IT HEADED OUT OVER THE NORTH ATLANTIC.

SUDDENLY, THE PLANE EXPLODED! BUCKY WAS KILLED INSTANTLY. BUT CAP WAS THROWN CLEAR OF THE EXPLOSION, PLUNGING INTO ICY ARCTIC WATERS.

THERE, THROUGH A FREAK ACCIDENT, HE WAS FROZEN INTO A STATE OF SUSPENDED ANIMATION. DECADES PASSED...

...AND FINALLY, CAP'S BODY WAS FOUND BY A NEW SUPER-TEAM WHICH HAD COME INTO BEING... A TEAM CALLED *THE AVENGERS!*

THEY VIEWED THEIR FIND WITH AWE, FOR MANY OF THE AVENGERS HAD FOUND INSPIRATION IN THE HISTORY-MAKING EXPLOITS OF THIS RED-WHITE-AND-BLUE LEGEND!

AND THEY WERE EVEN MORE AWED TO DISCOVER THAT CAP WAS NOT DEAD! THE LEGEND LIVED! AND HE SOON TOOK HIS PLACE AMONG THEM, OFTTIMES AS LEADER!

BUT STILL, EVEN AS AN AVENGER, HE WAS A MAN DECADES OUT OF TIME. AND IN THE MONTHS THAT FOLLOWED, STEVE ROGERS STROVE TO FIND A PLACE FOR HIMSELF IN THIS BRAVE NEW WORLD.

HE STROVE...AND SEARCHED... AND SUCCEEDED.

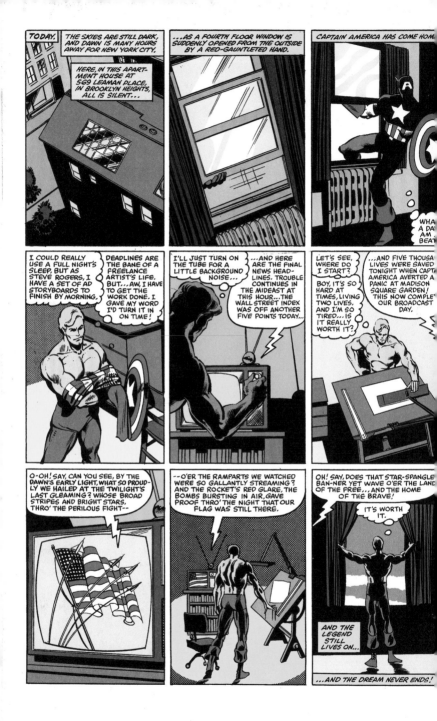